THE
JUNE
BABY

By Noel Streatfeild and available from Headline

The January Baby

The February Baby

The March Baby

The April Baby

The May Baby

The June Baby

The July Baby

The August Baby

The September Baby

The October Baby

The November Baby

The December Baby

THE

June

BABY

★

Noel Streatfeild

Copyright © Noel Streatfeild 1959
Copyright © The beneficiaries of the estate of Noel Streatfeild 1986
Excluding illustrations on pages v, 7, 8, 24, 28, 29, 55, 67,
70, 78, 83 © Becky Cameron 2023

The right of Noel Streatfeild to be identified as the Author of the Work has been
asserted by her in accordance with the Copyright, Designs and Patents Act 1988.

First published in 1959
This edition published in 2023 by Headline Home
an imprint of Headline Publishing Group

1

Apart from any use permitted under UK copyright law, this publication may
only be reproduced, stored, or transmitted, in any form, or by any means, with prior
permission in writing of the publishers or, in the case of reprographic production,
in accordance with the terms of licences issued by the Copyright Licensing Agency.

Every effort has been made to fulfil requirements with regard to reproducing copyright material.
The author and publisher will be glad to rectify any omissions at the earliest opportunity.

Cataloguing in Publication Data is available from the British Library

Hardback ISBN 978 1 0354 0849 8
eISBN 978 1 0354 0850 4

Typeset in 14.75/15pt Centaur MT Pro by Jouve (UK), Milton Keynes

Printed and bound in Great Britain by Clays Ltd, Elcograf S.p.A.

MIX
Paper | Supporting
responsible forestry
FSC® C104740

Headline's policy is to use papers that are natural, renewable and recyclable
products and made from wood grown in well-managed forests and other
controlled sources. The logging and manufacturing processes are expected
to conform to the environmental regulations of the country of origin.

HEADLINE PUBLISHING GROUP
An Hachette UK Company
Carmelite House
50 Victoria Embankment
London EC4Y 0DZ

www.headline.co.uk
www.hachette.co.uk

CONTENTS

This book contains examples of historical cures and home remedies. These are included for historical interest only and should not be followed. If your child is unwell, consult a doctor or other medical professional. Neither the author nor the publisher accept any liability for any loss or damage caused by the application of any of the information or suggestions in this book.

W HO if they could choose would not be a June baby? Who would not like to celebrate their early birthdays at strawberry picnics in a hay field? Now your June baby is here, the telephones have buzzed, and the good news has spread from friend to friend, especially the important part 'Mother and child are doing well.' The moment has now arrived when visitors are permitted, and everyone that you know is asking

themselves 'What present shall I bring her?'

The trouble with June is there are almost too many flowers. Roses, both from the shops and the garden, have probably been pouring in since your baby arrived. The less considerate have probably presented enormous sprays of lupins and delphiniums, exquisite to look at, but after the shortest time in water liable to break the heart of the stoutest-hearted nurse: never were flowers so disobliging in the way they

strew their unwanted petals on the floor. It is a temptation to bring yet more flowers, but the thoughtful will look for something else, because there must come a moment when vases give out, and a weary voice says 'They are lovely, but where, oh where, am I to put them?'

The right thing to bring the mother of the June baby is something for the baby to wear. But there are very few friends and relations

who are sufficiently strong minded to keep
the shawl they have knitted, or the little
frock they bought at the bazaar, or the
exquisite little matinee jacket they found in
France, until the baby has actually arrived.
'The last months of waiting before the baby
arrives are so trying,' everybody says, 'I shall
post her my parcel now.' This is partly an
honest desire to give pleasure, but also
impatience to hear the squeaks of admiration
over the telephone when the parcel has been
opened.

What most relations and friends long to buy is a toy. It is a most extraordinary thing, but there never seems to be the right

moment to present the most endearing toys. That pale blue monkey with the sad green eyes, that breaks your heart every time you pass it in the shop, should be a perfect present, but does the mother of the June baby really want a pale blue monkey with sad green eyes? And it is certain the baby could not care less.

Then what about something for the mother to wear? June is the perfect month to present the flimsiest of bed-jackets, or of course one of those exquisite two-piece affairs, of a nightdress with a matching negligée. Unfortunately, June is famous for other things besides roses, and one of them is that it includes a quarter day. It is sad as the Chancellor of the Exchequer gets tougher, how few friends can come staggering in carrying dainty boxes, full of diaphanous nonsense.

It is facing this problem of what shall I bring her, that has resulted in this book. Years of experience of visiting mothers with new babies, has taught me that there is only one subject about which either father or mother will talk, and that is the new baby. Here then, between two covers, is collected every sort of information about June babies of the past, and the present.

Very few parents need help in choosing names. Usually there are far too many names to choose from, there are grandparents to placate, and godfathers and godmothers, and that splendid old great-aunt who has a lot of

money, but no one knows to whom she is leaving it. But nevertheless occasionally parents, pink to the ears, arrive at the font still uncertain what they will answer when asked 'What name do you give this child?' For such parents here is a collection of names all in some way connected with June, from which they can choose.

No book which has anything to do with babies would be complete without the signs of the zodiac, and a description of the type of person who is supposed to be born under them. But in this book the pages on the zodiac signs are followed by a selection of people who were born on each day of June. Studying this may cause doubts to arise; had Henrietta Stuart, Duchess of Orleans really the attributes of Stan Laurel? And who would expect to find Henry VIII and Pirandello sharing a birthday? All the same, meditating on the signs of the zodiac under which your baby is born, can amuse if nothing else, and so too it is hoped you will find entertainment in reading of some others who share your baby's birthday.

NAMES
for the
JUNE
BABY

ALTHOUGH *June* is a popular name for those born at this time, few remember that it comes from *Juno* the Roman goddess, wife of Jupiter, and queen of heaven. Thinking of queens the name *Regina* means 'queen', and these names all mean 'the heavens', *Celia, Celine, Lilian* and *Lillian. Estella, Estelle, Esther, Stella* and *Vashti* all mean 'star'. From star it is only a short step to *Dawn,* and *Aurora* or *Zora* which mean the same thing, (but unexpectedly *Aurea* and *Aurelia* mean 'golden').

Juno was also bringer of light, so how about *Lucina, Lucia, Lucilia, Lucilla, Lucinda, Lucy* and *Selina* which mean 'light'. As well Juno was protectress of women, and it was the custom to pray to her during childbirth; *Natalia* and *Natalie* mean 'birth'. While you are thinking about the Roman gods, did you know that *Pagan* was a popular boy's name, but not until after the Norman Conquest? It died out during the Reformation, but it would be fun to revive it.

The birthstone for June is the pearl, which is a pretty name, and if you prefer another name that means 'pearl' you can choose from *Greta, Maisie, Margaret, Margery, Margot, Marguerite, Marjorie, Marjory* or *Rita*.

Roses are flowering everywhere in June. Apart from *Rose: Rosa, Rosetta, Rosina* and *Rosita* all have the same meaning. *Rosabel* and *Rosabella* mean 'pretty rose', *Rosalind* and *Rosaline* 'fair as a rose', *Rosamond* and *Rosamund* 'pure rose' and *Rhoda* 'rose bush'.

Every month in the year has an apostle dedicated to it. St Thomas belongs to June, and his name means 'twin'.

There are a fair number of special days in June.

The 1st of June is the day of St Conrad. *Conrad* means 'bold counsel'.

The 3rd of June is dedicated to St Cecil. *Cecil* is as suitable for a girl as for a boy.

St Boniface's Day is on the 5th of June. *Boniface* means 'well-doer'.

St Norbert's Day is the 6th of June. *Norbert*, if it has a meaning, means 'Niord's brightness'.

The 11th of June is St Barnaby's Day. *Barnaby* means 'son of consolation' and so does *Barnabas*.

The 14th of June is the day of Basil the Great. *Basil*, besides being the name of a herb, means 'kingly' and so does *Tiernan*. *Blaise* and *Blaze* mean 'royal', *Cornelius* 'regal', *Melchior* 'king of light' and *Rex* is another word for 'king'.

St Alban's Day is the 17th of June. *Alban* means 'white', and so does *Albany*.

Magna Carta 1215 is one of the few dates in history which most people remember, but who knows it was signed on the 19th of June? It might be an idea to look at the names of some of the people who were present on that great occasion. Besides King John, there are *Stephen*, which means 'crown', *Henry* 'home ruler', *William* 'resolute helmet', *Jocelin* or *Joscelin* 'merry', *Hugh* or *Hugo* 'mind', *Walter* 'ruling the folk', *Benedict* 'blessed', *Alan*, *Allan* or *Allen* 'harmony', *Hubert* 'of bright mind', *Matthew* 'gift of Jehovah', *Thomas* 'twin', *Philip* 'horse-lover', and *Robert*, *Robin* or *Rupert* 'bright fame'.

Amongst the barons who were siding against King John at this time were *Richard* which means 'stern ruler', *Geoffrey* 'district-peace', *Roger* 'spear of fame', *Eustace* 'fruitful', *Ralph* 'counsel-wolf', *Simon* 'hearkening', *Oliver* 'olive tree', *Humphrey* 'giant peace', *Theobald* 'folk-bold', *Nicholas* or *Nicol* 'victory of the people', and *Alexander, Alec, Alex, Alick, Alastair, Alistair, Alister, Sander* and *Saunder* all mean 'defending men'. *Magna* is the Latin word for 'great,' and might suit either a boy or a girl.

Midsummer's Eve is on the 23rd of June. All over the world legends have grown up about the magical gifts bestowed on June babies. The most popular and widely held is that a child born on Midsummer's Eve can, at midnight on that day, see and talk to the fairies. So *Fay*, which means 'fairy', would be a good name for a Midsummer's Eve baby. And while we are thinking of fairies, *Gloriana* means 'queen of the fairies' and *Gloria* 'glory'.

From fairies it is a natural jump to Queen Mab, spoken of in Shakespeare's plays. *Mab* is short for *Mabel*, which means 'fairy', and so do *Amabel*, *Annabel* and *Annabella*. A Midsummer Night's Dream suggests *Hermia* or *Hermione* which mean 'daughter of Hermes' or *Helena* 'bright one'. *Titania* was another name for *Diana*, the Roman goddess of chastity.

The 24th of June is St John the Baptist's Day. *John* means 'the Lord's Grace'; other

forms of this name are *Iain, Ian, Ivan, Jack, Jon, Sean, Shane* and *Shawn.*

St Peter's Day is the 29th of June; he shares his day with St Paul. *Peter* means 'stone', *Stanley* means 'stony meadow' and *Wystan* 'battle-stone'. *Paul* means 'little'.

The 30th of June is St Bertram's Day. *Bertram* means 'bright raven'.

June is of course the month of roses, and *Rose* is a charming name, but it is fun to leave you with an unusual flower name to think about. How about *Syringa*, with its orange blossom scented sprays? what could be prettier or more original for a baby girl?

GIFTS
for the
JUNE
BABY

IF any godparent or well-wisher would like to give a piece of jewellery to the June baby, the right stone is the pearl, which is the emblem of purity and innocence. Mothers of baby girls will probably sigh and think back to the days when sometimes a pearl necklace was started as a christening present – with a few real pearls threaded on a chain, and a promise that pearls would be added each birthday and Christmas, until the girl's twenty-first birthday when the necklace would be complete. But few babies are given such presents today. All the same pearls in some form will come the child's way, so here is what Leonardus has to say about them in *The Mirror of Stones*, published in 1750:

'. . . being boil'd in Meat they cure the Quartan Ague; bruised and taken with Milk they heal putrid Ulcers; and being so taken wonderfully clear the Voice. They comfort the Heart, and give Relief in Pains of the Stomach, and remove the Epilepsy; they stop the Flux of the Belly; if taken with Sugar, they yield Help in pestilential Fevers; and render him who carries them chaste.'

So if your June baby should at any time lose her voice, she will know what to do with any pearls she may possess.

The pretty old custom of knowing how to arrange flowers in a vase or bunch so that it brings a message, is neglected nowadays. If however, your baby should receive a bunch of roses and honeysuckle, the message says:

Love (roses) and generous devoted affection (honeysuckle).

If your baby was born between the 1st and the 21st of June read pages 24 and 25, but if between the 22nd and the, 30th skip to pages 26 and 27.

UNDER
WHAT STARS WAS
MY BABY
BORN?

GEMINI
The Twins
22nd May–21st June

CANCER
The Crab
22nd June–23rd July

LEO
The Lion
24th July–23rd August

VIRGO
The Virgin
24th August–23rd September

LIBRA
The Scales
24th September–23rd October

SCORPIO
The Scorpion
24th October–22nd November

SAGITTARIUS
The Archer

23rd November–21st December

CAPRICORN
The Sea Goat

22nd December–20th January

AQUARIUS
The Water Bearer

21st January–19th February

PISCES
The Fishes

20th February–20th March

ARIES
The Ram

21st March–20th April

TAURUS
The Bull

21st April–21st May

Gemini — the Twins
22nd May—21st June

THE distinguishing characteristic of people born under Gemini is intellectual brilliance. They are intuitive as well as observant and are always fond of the arts or sciences. Their understanding of human relationships is swift and sure, though they are apt themselves to be but superficial participants. Gemini people are generally quick and active, even nervous, restless and changeable. They are subtle, perhaps devious. Their conversation is animated, and rich in vocabulary. They need usually to cultivate in their lives a sense of continuity and purpose.

For the Gemini Baby

Lucky to wear topaz, amber, zireen.
Lucky stones are marble, glass.
Lucky metal is quicksilver.
The Gemini baby's colour is yellow.
Lucky number is 5.
Luckiest day is Wednesday.

Cancer — the Crab
22nd June–23rd July

People born under Cancer are magnetic and receptive. Themselves rather self-contained, they draw others to them, and are tenacious in relationships where their strong protective instinct is appealed to strongly enough to turn their will to personal aggrandisement into kindness, sympathy and understanding. Cancer people are reflective, but somewhat uncommunicative. They have orderly habits and low, soft voices. Their forte is parenthood: they make better fathers and mothers than people of any other sign.

For the Cancer Baby

Lucky to wear pearls, moonstone, cats-eye, aquamarine.
Lucky stone is crystal.
Lucky metal is silver.
The Cancer baby's colour is turquoise.
Lucky numbers are 2 and 7.
Luckiest day is Monday.

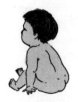

BABIES BORN
ON
THE SAME DAY
AS
YOUR BABY

IS there any truth in what the astrologers say: that babies born under Gemini are like this and those born under Cancer are like that? If you read through the following list you will see some of the well-known people who were born on each day in June, and it may make you wonder if the astrologers are right.

1st   Robert Cecil, Earl of Salisbury, 1560. Karl von Clausewitz, 1780. John Masefield, 1878. Robert Newton, 1905. Sir Frank Whittle, 1907. Marilyn Monroe, 1926.

2nd   Marquis de Sade, 1740. Glinka, 1803. Pope Pius X, 1835. Thomas Hardy, 1840. Sir Edward Elgar, 1857.

3rd   Henry Shrapnel, 1761. Richard Cobden, 1804. George V, 1865. Raoul

Dufy, 1877. Josephine Baker, 1906. Paulette Goddard, 1911. Françoise Arnoul, 1931.

4th   George III, 1738. Field Marshal Viscount Wolseley, 1833. Gustaf Mannerheim, 1867. Dr Frank Buchman, 1878.

5th   Socrates, 468 B.C. Edmund Langley, Duke of York, 1341. Adam Smith, 1723. Ernest Augustus, King of Hanover, 1771. Jean Cocteau, 1889.

6th   Velasquez, 1599. Corneille, 1606. Pushkin, 1799. Scott of the Antarctic, 1868. Thomas Mann, 1875. Dame Ninette de Valois, 1898.

7th   John Rennie, 1761. Robert Jenkinson, Earl of Liverpool, 1770. Beau Brummell, 1778. R. D. Blackmore, 1825. Carlotta, Empress of Mexico, 1840. Gauguin, 1848. Elizabeth Bowen, 1899.

8th   Cagliostro, 1743. Robert Schuman, 1810. Charles Reade, 1814. Sir John Everett Millais, 1829. Frank Lloyd Wright, 1869.

9th   Peter the Great of Russia, 1672. George Stephenson, 1781. Viscount Brookeborough, 1888. Cole Porter, 1893.

10th Prince James Edward, 'The Old Pretender,' 1688. Terence Rattigan, 1911. Duke of Edinburgh, 1921. Judy Garland, 1922.

11th John Constable, 1776. Gerard Manley Hopkins, 1844. Dame Millicent Fawcett, 1847. Mrs Humphry Ward, 1851. Richard Todd, 1919. Beryl Grey, 1927.

12th Harriet Martineau, 1802. Charles Kingsley, 1819. Viscountess Rhondda, 1833. Julia Neilson, 1869. Sir Anthony Eden, 1897. Norman Hartnell, 1901.

13th Agricola, A.D. 46. Philip 'The Good,' Duke of Burgundy, 1396. Fanny Burney, 1752. William Lilly-white, 1792.

W. B. Yeats, 1865. Basil Rathbone, 1892. Prince Aly Khan, 1911.

14th   Harriet Beecher Stowe, 1811. John McCormack, 1884. Sam Wanamaker, 1919.

15th   Edward 'The Black Prince,' 1330. Anthony Francis de Fourcroy, 1755. Edvard Grieg, 1843. Belinda Lee, 1935.

16th   Henrietta Stuart, Duchess of Orleans, 1644. Louis, Duc de Saint-Simon, 1675. Gustav V of Sweden, 1858. Stan Laurel, 1890.

17th   Edward I, 1239. Gounot, 1818. Stravinsky, 1882. G. B. Stern, 1890.

18th   Viscount Castlereagh, 1769. Ian Carmichael, 1920.

19th   James I, 1566. Pascal, 1623. Earl Haig, 1861. W. R. Hammond, 1903. Pier Angeli, 1932.

20th   Offenbach, 1819. John Aloysius Costello, 1891. Dr Heinrich von Brentano, 1904. Rupert Croft-Cooke, 1904. Rosanna Podesta, 1934.

21st   Field-Marshal Sir Claude Auchinleck, 1884. Jean-Paul Sartre, 1905. Françoise Sagan, 1935.

22nd   Mazzini, 1805. Sir H. Rider Haggard,
        1856. Puccini, 1858. Dr Julian Huxley,
        1887. Sir John Hunt, 1910.
23rd   Josephine, Empress of the French, 1763.
        Duke of Windsor, 1894. Alfred Charles
        Kinsey, 1894. Jean Anouilh, 1910. Sir
        Len Hutton, 1916.
24th   Robert Dudley, Earl of Leicester, 1532.
        John the Baptist, 1542. Duke of
        Marlborough, 1650. Sir John Ross,
        1777. Lord Kitchener, 1850.
25th   Beatrice, Duchess of Bretagne, 1242.
        Earl Mountbatten, 1900. Esther
        McCracken, 1902.
26th   George Morland, 1763. Lord Kelvin,
        1824. Pearl Buck, 1892.
27th   Louis XII ('The Just') of France, 1462.
        Charles IX of France, 1550. Charles
        XII of Sweden, 1682. Muriel Pavlow,
        1921. C. S. Parnell, 1846.
28th   Henry VIII, 1491. John Wesley, 1703.
        Jean Jacques Rousseau, 1712. Charles
        Mathews, 1776. Luigi Pirandello, 1867.
        Eric Ambler, 1909.
29th   Rubens, 1577. Leopardi, 1798. Count
        Witte, 1849.

30th Comte de Barras, 1755. Thomas Lovell Beddoes, 1803. Sir Joseph Dalton Hooker, 1817. Alfred Austen, 1835. Harold Laski, 1893. Susan Hayward, 1917.

THE UPBRINGING OF JUNE BABIES OF THE PAST

IT is grievously to be lamented, that so many Mothers, not only of high Rank, but even of the common Sort, can with so much Inhumanity, and more than brutish Cruelty, desert their tender Offspring, and expose them to so many Dangers of mercenary Nurses, who are greedy only of the profuse Rewards bestowed on them at the Christening, and slight the small weekly Income that follows; and so being weary of the present Employment, perform it negligently, while they are looking out for a new Prey. But let us take a Survey of the Advantages that prompt Mothers so commonly to sacrifice their beloved Offspring. They are the more free Enjoyment of Diversions; the greater Niceness of adorning their Persons; the Opportunity of receiving impertinent Visits, and returning those insipid Favours; the more frequent Attendance on the Theatre, or the spending the greatest Part of the Night on their beloved Cards. These are the important Reasons, for which Mothers frequently banish their new-born Infants from their Sight, and rashly deliver them up into very doubtful Hands, whithersoever Fortune or Fate, either good or bad, happens to lead them. But these nice Ladies afterwards suffer deserved Punishments; for the Love of their Children, if they happen to survive, is more cool towards them, but warm and affectionate towards the Nurse who took them up, and performed the Duties of a real Mother.

1742.

In Turkey when a child is born it is immediately laid in the cradle and loaded with amulets, and a small bit of soft mud, well steeped in a jar of water, properly prepared by previous charms, is stuck upon its forehead, to obviate the effects of the evil eye. This fascination is feared at all times, and is supposed to affect people of all ages, who by their prosperity may be the objects of envy. Not only a Greek, but a Turkish woman, on seeing a stranger look eagerly at her child, will spit in its face; and sometimes if at herself, in her own bosom; but the use of garlic, or even of the word which signifies that herb, is considered a sovereign preventive.

Hobhouse, *Travels*, 1813.

RICKETS

CAUSES. The *remote* or *inducing* are, bad nursing – suckling children too long – an acid produced from the milk with which the child is fed for the first nine months, or feeding it on unfermented farinaceous substances, and indulging too much in their use, particularly such aliments as possess too firm a texture, and are too viscid and sour, as bread not well fermented, cheese, cheese-cakes, garden fruits – giving children sour wine – living in bad air, or low marshy places – opiates too frequently and freely given, want of proper exercise – the habit weakened by preceding diseases – a diseased nurse – and external violence.

The *proximate* or *immediate*, a *torpid state of the circulatory system*, and *general flaccidity or relaxation of the solids preternaturally increased*, by which the organs of digestion, assimilation, and nutrition, are defective in their power, and bring on a thin state of fluids, and want of that matter, called *ossific*, in them, which form the bones.

•　　•　　•　　•　　•

CURE. The chief tonics employed in these cases are bark and steel . . .

Culpeper, 1802.

The first cries of children are intreaties; if we take no notice of them, they soon fall into the imperative strain; they begin with begging our assistance, they conclude with commanding our obedience. Thus even from their weakness, which gives them the first notion of their dependance, arises the idea of empire and dominion: but this idea not being awaked so much by their wants, as by our services, here they begin to perceive the moral effects, the immediate cause of which is not founded in nature; and hence we see why, in this early stage, it behoves us to discover the private intention, by which the gesture or cry is directed.

When the child extends its hand with some effort, but without speaking, he thinks to reach the object, because he does not estimate the distance; but he is mistaken: when he complains and cries at the same time that he extends his hand, then he is not mistaken as to the distance, but commands the object to approach, or you to bring it towards him. In the former case,

lead him to the object slowly and by degrees;
in the latter, do not seem as if you so much as
heard him; the more he cries, the less ought
you to mind his importunity. It is a matter of
consequence to accustom him betimes, neither
to command men, for he is not their master;
nor things, for they do not understand his
command. Therefore when a child desires a
thing he sees, and which you intend to give
him, it is much preferable to lead him to the
object, than to bring the object to him; from
thence he draws a conclusion suited to his own
age, and there is no possibility of suggesting it
to him any other way.

Rousseau, 1763.

I believe giving children beer, or wine, or spirits
and water, with the idea of strengthening them,
is a pernicious custom. The delicate coats

43

of their stomachs get injured by fermented liquors, and in consequence of this, an unnatural craving is excited, and many, when grown up, have in consequence taken to drinking. I of course except cases where medical men order such stimulants; but unless absolutely necessary, I would advise them not to be given. Another most injurious custom is that of giving children sips of wine when they come into the dining-room after dinner. Wine was given 'to make glad the heart of *man*,' but not that of *children*; it only makes them sorrowful.

Kingston, *Infant Amusements*, 1867.

A GOOD POWDER FOR MARASMUS OF CHILDREN

Seventeen good pearls, thirteen corals, a chicken stomach, a sprig of green rosemary, green marjoram, nine palsy grains, three sprigs of mouse-ear herbs.

Albertus Magnus, *White and Black Art for Man and Beast*, 13th C., trans. c. 1880.

The slow and temperate Heat of a young Child requires a moderate Exercise, like a gentle Gale of Wind, to rouze and quicken him, and to enable him the better to perform his natural Functions: Wherefore his first Exercise is to be rock'd, laid along in his Cradle, which, for that End, is suspended or plac'd upon a Pedestal or Foot, turn'd half round in a Semicircle; or else being held in Arms, he is shaked up and down, or from one Side to the other; this is done very gently if it be soon after he has suck'd, but a little more strongly, if it be some Time after. When he is grown a little, that is to say, about the second or third Month, he may be allow'd the Use of his Hands, but so that his Left-Hand may always be less at Liberty than his Right; for fear, lest by using it too often, it should grow stronger, and more easy for him to use than his Right, and so he should become Left-handed. When he is a little older, he may be drawn in a little Waggon to exercise his whole Body. He should not be oblig'd to walk alone too soon, for fear of making his Feet or Legs turn either

inward or outward, or his Feet grow flat:
But when his Limbs begin to grow strong
and nervous, from the Use of some good
and substantial Diet, it will be Time to
make him begin to go alone. Then his
Nurse ought to support him by his
Leading-Strings, 'till he is able to put his
Feet upon the Ground, and rest himself
upon them. In short, in order to accustom
him to go alone, he should be shut up in a
little Go-Cart, or Go-Wain, which will roll
him on as he goes, without any Danger of
falling; and most Children are wonderfully
pleas'd and delighted with this Kind of
Exercise.

The Nurse's Guide, by an Eminent
Physician, London: 1729.

CURE FOR MEASLES. — My nurse declared that I and my brother and sister were cured of the above by having some hair cut from the nape of each of our necks, and then separately placed between two slices of bread and butter. She says she watched anxiously for a strange dog to pass (no other being efficacious). She then gave him the bread and butter, and as he ate it without loathing, she was sure we should be cured. He went away, and of course never came again, for *he* died of the measles — miserably, no doubt, poor fellow, having travelled off with the disease of three affected children!

A Correspondent, in *Notes and Queries*, 1855.

Necklaces of Peony-root, worn by children, prevent convulsions.

Folkard, *Plant Lore*, 1884.

It seems now more like a tradition of the elders, than a thing of actual occurrence, when we recall the fashion of the early part of the present century, in regard to an infant's head gear. First, a flannel cap, fitting close to

47

the head, and over this a cambric or muslin one, with innumerable frills, standing out all around the poor little wrinkled-up face. The under cap was rarely changed, and when the time came for it to be dispensed with, the careful nurse cut it away in portions, *a little at a time*, lest the baby should take cold by the sudden change. This precaution – worthy of the age of flannel rollers – any sensible person will see at once the injudicious care, which kept the child's head in a continual vapor bath.

Then came the custom of the outside cap alone, an unnecessary bit of expense and trouble, to say nothing of more serious disadvantages, entirely done away with in the past ten years.

Now, caps are only used in an out-of-door dress, or when the child is carried across passages, as from the nursery to the parlor. It is not necessary to provide more than one at first, and this is usually made a gift – nursery presents, for a first child especially, being as fashionable as bridal offerings. If the little thing goes out before it is six weeks old (and many physicians recommend daily exercise in the open air after the third week), it can be wrapped, ears and all, in a hood blanket, over a close, simple, little lace cap, lined with soft Florence silk, with a narrow ruche of blonde net; any mother can manufacture one sufficiently elegant.

The Nursery Basket, New York, 1854.

HOOPING COUGH. — A gentleman, whom I met the other day at a dinner party in the country, told me that in some parts of Yorkshire 'owl broth' is considered a specific; and that he had shot these birds several times, at the request of cottagers, in order that they might be able to prepare it for children afflicted with hooping-cough.

A Correspondent, *Notes and Queries*, 1863.

TO PARENTS. — A Widow Lady of respect-ability, residing at North End, Croydon, feels inclined to take SIX or EIGHT CHILDREN, whose health requires air, and too weakly to bear the fatigues of a School. Should any Lady or Gentleman place confidence enough to trust her with their little charge, may rely on her parental care, having brought up a large family of her own, and well knows the litte ailments incident to children; can receive none under 4 years old. Particulars may be had by applying at No. 13, Aldgate; and 201, Bishopsgate street, London.

The Times, 1809.

A
ROYAL JUNE
BABY

JAMES THE FIRST OF ENGLAND
AND SIXTH OF SCOTLAND
born June 1566.

HIS conduct, at opening his parliament in 1571, when he had arrived at the discreet age of four years, stamps him at once as a juvenile oddity. In those days, good subjects were not contented without they identified the person of an infant king, by seeing him perform his regal duty of opening parliament. Accordingly, the lords and burgesses of Scotland convened at Stirling in the great hall of the castle, a noble gothic room, 120 feet in length. Thither the infant king was carried in the arms of his trusty guardian, the earl of Marr, and placed on the throne at the upper end, having been previously taught a short speech to repeat to his parliament. From the throne the little creature silently and curiously made his observations on the scene before him, and, among other things, espied a hole in the roof of the hall, where a slate had slipped off and admitted the light. Others say that the hole was in the canopy of the throne. However, when he was required to make his speech, he recited it with astonishing gravity and precision, but added to it, in the same tone, the result of his previous observation, in these words: 'There is *ane* hole in this parliament.'

Strickland, *Lives of the Queens of England*, 1875.

DISTINGUISHED
JUNE
BABIES

HARRIET MARTINEAU
born June 1802.

I KNOW nothing more strange than this power of re-entering, as it were, into the narrow mind of an infant, so as to compare it with that of maturity; and therefore it may be worth while to record that piece of precious nonsense, – my dream at four years old. I imagine I was learning my letters then from cards, where each letter had its picture, – as a stag for

S. I dreamed that we children were taking our walk with our nursemaid out of St Austin's Gate (the nearest bit of country to our house.) Out of the public-house there came a stag, with prodigious antlers. Passing the pump, it crossed the road to us, and made a polite bow, with its head on one side, and with a scrape of one foot, after which it pointed with its foot to the public-house, and spoke to me, inviting me in. The maid declined, and turned to go home. Then came the terrible part. By the time we were at our own door, it was dusk, and we went up the steps in the dark; but in the kitchen it was bright sunshine. My mother was standing at the dresser, breaking sugar; and she lifted me up, and set me in the sun, and gave me a bit of sugar. Such was the dream which froze me with horror! Who shall say why? – But my panics were really unaccountable. They were a matter of pure sensation, without any intellectual justification whatever, even of the wildest kind. A magic-lantern was exhibited to us on Christmas-day, and once or twice in the year besides. I used to see it cleaned by

daylight, and to handle all its parts, —
understanding its whole structure; yet, such
was my terror of the white circle on the
wall, and of the moving slides, that, to
speak the plain truth, the first apparition
always brought on bowel-complaint; and, at
the age of thirteen, when I was pretending
to take care of little children during the
exhibition, I could never look at it without
having the back of a chair to grasp, or
hurting myself, to carry off the intolerable
sensation. My bitter shame may be
conceived; but then, I was always in a state
of shame about something or other.

Harriet Martineau, *Autobiography*, 1877.

JEAN JACQUES ROUSSEAU
born June 1712.

I have no knowledge of what passed prior to
my fifth or sixth year; I recollect nothing of
learning to read, I only remember what
effect the first considerable exercise of it
produced on my mind; and from that
moment I date an uninterrupted knowledge
of myself.

Every night, after supper, we read some part of a small collection of romances which had been my mother's. My father's design was only to improve me in reading, and he thought these entertaining works were calculated to give me a fondness for it; but we soon found ourselves so interested in the adventures they contained, that we alternately read whole nights together, and could not bear to give over until at the conclusion of a volume. Sometimes, in a morning, on hearing the swallows at our window, my father, quite ashamed of this weakness, would cry, 'Come; come, let us go to bed; I am more a child than thou art.'

I soon acquired, by this dangerous custom, not only an extreme facility in reading and comprehending, but, for my age, a too intimate acquaintance with the passions. An infinity of sensations were familiar to me, without possessing any precise idea of the objects to which they related ... I had conceived nothing ... I had felt the whole. This confused succession of emotions did not retard the future efforts of my reason, though they added an extravagant, romantic notion of human life, which experience and reflection have never been able to eradicate.

The Confessions of J. J. Rousseau,
translated from the French, 1796.

GEORGE MORLAND
born June 1763.

A striking instance of that singularity of character which George Morland possessed throughout his life is contained in the following anecdote, the authenticity of which may be relied on . . . Mr West, the present celebrated president of the Royal Academy, called upon the senior Morland who had some pictures to clean for him, when George was only four years old, and found him in the painting-room with nothing but a dirty shirt on. The visitor spoke to him for some time without obtaining any answer; and at last he told him that he supposed he had no tongue. Young Morland instantly put out his tongue and grinned in his face; and his father coming in at the moment gave him a kick on the breech and sent him away, observing that he had

deeply studied his disposition, and knew
him to be so extraordinary a child, that he
would either be an eminent man or he would
come to the gallows.

Blagdon, *Memoirs of George Morland*, 1806.

CHARLES WATERTON
born June 1782.

My first adventure on the water made a
lasting impression, on account of the
catastrophe which attended it. There was a
large horsepond, separated by a hedge from
the field which was allotted to the scholars for
recreation-ground. An oblong tub, used for
holding dough before it is baked, had just
been placed by the side of the pond. I thought
that I could like to have an excursion on the
deep; so taking a couple of stakes out of the
hedge, to serve as oars, I got into the tub, and
pushed off . . . I had got above half way over,
when, behold, the master and the late Sir John
Lawson of Brough Hall, suddenly rounded a
corner and hove in sight. Terrified at their
appearance, I first lost a stake, and then my
balance: this caused the tub to roll like a

man-of-war in a calm. Down I went to the bottom, and rose again covered with mud and dirt . . . My good old master looked grave, and I read my destiny in his countenance; but Sir John said that it was a brave adventure, and he saved me from being brought to a court-martial for disobedience of orders, and for having lost my vessel.

Waterton, *Essays on Natural History*, 1838.

BEAU BRUMMELL
born June 1778.

This formerly fashionable authority in all things connected with the external decencies of society, was, when a boy, as afterwards when a man, a greedy, selfish, empty, conceited coxcomb, whose luck it was in life to meet with greater fools than himself; and by bullying them into a notion of his superiority, to cajole and direct them. At the dinner-table of the old lady he gave a good specimen of the physical greediness of his nature and the essential vulgarity of his disposition. Having stuffed himself almost to bursting with the viands of the feast, he actually burst into tears, and sobbingly regretted that his belly could not stretch itself to dimensions commensurate with his desire to gormandize. The admirers, imitators, and pupils of this precious coxcomb may feel astonished at this passage in his career. They may, nevertheless, rely upon the truth of it; it is vouched for by one who knew him well.

Rev. J. Richardson, *Recollections*, 1856.

CHARLES MATHEWS
born June 1776.

This fellow's regular cry was, 'Live eels! Conger eels! Thames eels! – try my eels – silver eels – Dutch eels – threepence a pound e-e-e-e-e-els!' which, taking a fresh supply of breath from his leathern lungs, he *eel*-longated to such an extent, that the last monosyllable frequently held out in undimished force and energy while he strided from Craven to Hungerford Street.

An imitation of this odd, perambulating fish-monger, I considered as most desirable. He was a notorious character, and excited various laughs, from the infant snigger to the adult roar; and 'What a long eel!' was the constant remark his drollery excited. Even my father's serious friends relaxed so far from their rigidity of muscle as to ha-ha-ha nearly three times at my successful hitting off of his peculiarities. Encouraged by this approbation into boldness, having brought my parody to perfection, I was emulous of the approval of the great original himself; and having due notice of his approach from the long eel on which he was trilling perhaps as far off as Charing Cross, I anxiously awaited his arrival. When he was near enough to observe my action, I placed my hand on the dexter side of my mouth, and commenced my sinister operations, taking him off 'to the very life', as my panegyrists had led me to believe I could. Had I been as slippery as one of his own articles of traffic I might have twisted and wriggled my way behind the counter and escaped; but he was too much for me – indeed I did not apprehend so savage an attack. Deliberately placing his basket at the door, he pursued me into the shop; and as I flinched from the huge and ponderous fist that was poised high in air to annihilate me, I conveniently placed my back to receive his blow. 'Next time,' said the huge monster as he felled me to the earth, 'as you twists your little wry mouth about and cuts your mugs at a respectable tradesman, I'll skin you like an e-e-' and seizing his whole shop up in his Brobdignagian arms, he finished the monosyllable somewhere about No. 27. For weeks – nay, months – did I suffer from the effects of this punishment.'

Memoirs of Charles Mathews, London, 1838.

GAMES
for the
JUNE
BABY

THERE was a great deal of equestrian exercise in the old nursery, the knee being the ever-ready substitute for a horse. Here is one of the appropriate rhymes:

> I had a little pony,
>   They ca'd it Dapple Grey;
> I lent it to a lady,
>   To ride a mile away.
>
> She whipt it, she lash'd it,
>   She ca'd it ower the brae;
> I winna lend my pony mair,
>   Though a' the ladies pray.
>
> _Popular Rhymes of Scotland_,
> W. & R. Chambers, 1842.

RING O' ROSES. A ring, moving round, till the last line, when they stand and imitate sneezing.
Chorus.   'A ring, a ring o' roses,
                A pocket-full o' posies;

68

One for Jack and one for Jim
and one for little Moses!
A-tisha! a-tisha! a-tisha!'
Jackson, *Shropshire Folk-Lore*, 1883.

HOOPS. – The use of hoops should be especially encouraged. Strong, narrow hoops are the best, that is to say like the wheel of a gig, rather than that of a broad-wheeled waggon. The hoop-stick should have a flat blade and a round handle, and should be of sufficient length to save the child from knocking its knuckles. The hoop should be pressed against it, rather than struck hard, as is usually done. Children will thus soon learn not only to drive their hoops straight forward, but to twist and turn them about in every direction.
Kingston, *Infant Amusements*, 1867.

A JUNE
CHILD IN
FICTION

CERTAINLY, she had ways with her such as I never saw a child take up before; and she put all of us past our patience fifty times and oftener in a day: from the hour she came downstairs till the hour she went to bed, we had not a minute's security that she wouldn't be in mischief. Her spirits were always at high-water mark, her tongue always going – singing, laughing, and plaguing everybody who would not do the same. A wild, wicked slip she was – but she had the bonniest eye, the sweetest smile, and lightest foot in the parish: and, after all, I believe she meant no harm; for when once she made you cry in good earnest, it seldom happened that she would not keep you company, and oblige you to be quiet that you might comfort her.

She was much too fond of Heathcliff. The greatest punishment we could invent for her was to keep her separate from him; yet she got chided more than any of us on his account.

In play, she liked exceedingly to act the little mistress; using her hands freely, and commanding her companions: she did so to me, but I would not bear shopping and ordering; and so I let her know.

Now, Mr Earnshaw did not understand jokes from his children; he had always been strict and grave with them; and Catherine, on her part, had no idea why her father should be crosser and less patient in his ailing condition, than he was in his prime.

His peevish reproofs wakened in her a naughty delight to provoke him: she was never so happy as when we were all scolding her at once, and she defying us with her bold, saucy look, and her ready words; turning Joseph's religious curses into ridicule, baiting me, and doing just what her father hated most – showing how her pretended insolence, which he thought real, had more power over Heathcliff than his kindness: how the boy would do *her* bidding in anything, and *his* only when it suited his own inclination.

Emily Brontë, *Wuthering Heights*, 1847.

Tommy was taught hymns, very soon after he could speak, appropriate to his tender age, pointing out to him the inevitable fate of wicked children, and giving him the earliest possible warning and description of the punishment of little sinners. He repeated these poems to his stepmother after dinner, before a great, shining mahogany table, covered with grapes, pineapples, plum-cake, port wine, and Madeira, and surrounded by stout men in black, with baggy white neckcloths, who took the little man between their knees, and questioned him as to his right understanding of the place whither naughty boys were bound. They patted his head with their fat hands if he said well, or rebuked him if he was bold, as he often was.

Thackeray, *The Newcomes*, 1855.

LETTERS
from
JUNE
CHILDREN

GEORGE V as Duke of York, aged six, to a Lady, 1871.

I am writing with your lovely ink and thank you so much for bringing it down last night, it was so very kind. We went yesterday to see Grandmama's swords pistols guns the bullet in a locket that killed Nelson the sword full of arrows tigers and peacocks and stars. We will write with this ink to Mama tomorrow.

... We were photographed twice yesterday and the day before the man took a long time ... GEORGE.

Princess Louisa Maria, daughter of James II and Mary of Modena, born 28th June, 1692, to her Mother.

Madame,

I hope that this letter will find your majesty in as good health as when I left you. I am at present quite well, but I was very tired after my journey. I am very glad to learn from my brother that you are well. I desire extremely your majesty's return, which I hope will be tomorrow evening, between seven and eight o'clock. M. Caryl begs me to inquire of you if I ought to sign my letter to the nuncio 'Louise Marie, P.' I am impatient to learn if you have had any tidings of the king.

I am, madame,

Your majesty's very humble
and obedient daughter,
LOUISE MARIE.
St G., this 21st of May, 1700.

Charles Kingsley, later author of *The Water Babies* (1862), to a friend of his parents, who had become an object of his childish affection.

Barnack.

My dear Miss Dade,

I hope you are well is fanny well? The house is completely changed since you went. I think it is nearly 3 months since you went. Mamma sends her love to you and sally browne Herbert and geraled but I must stop here, because I

have more letters of consequenece to write &
here I must pause.

    Believe me always, Your sincere friend,
             Charles Kingsley.
                   (At the age of 5 or 6.)

RHYMES
for the
JUNE
BABY

JUNE brings tulips, lilies, roses,
Fills the children's hands with posies.
                    Sara Coleridge (1802–1852).

A BOY'S SONG

Where the pools are bright and deep,
Where the grey trout lies asleep,
Up the river and o'er the lea,
That's the way for Billy and me.

Where the blackbird sings the latest,
Where the hawthorn blooms the sweetest,
Where the nestlings chirp and flee,
That's the way for Billy and me.

Where the mowers mow the cleanest,
Where the hay lies thick and greenest,
There to trace the homeward bee,
That's the way for Billy and me.

Where the hazel bank is steepest,
Where the shadow falls the deepest,
Where the clustering nuts fall free,
That's the way for Billy and me.

Why the boys should drive away
Little sweet maidens from the play,
Or love to banter and fight so well,
That's the thing I never could tell.

But this I know, I love to play,
Through the meadow, among the hay;
Up the water and o'er the lea,
That's the way for Billy and me.

James Hogg (1770–1835).

Sleep, my child, sleep my child,
Where is thy nurse gone?
She is gone to the mountains
To buy thee sweetmeats.
What shall she buy thee?
The thundering drum, the bamboo pipe,
The trundling man, or the paper kite.

Child-life in Japan,
by M. Chaplin Ayrton, 1879.

A PRAYER

Lord, teach a little child to pray,
   And fill my heart with love,
And make me fitter every day
   To go to heaven above.

O hear my little simple prayer,
   My faults and sins forgive,
That I may join the angels there,
   And with my Saviour live.

Short and Simple Prayers,
London: 1844.

GOODNIGHT
to the
JUNE BABY

IF June is behaving itself it is a warm night, and your window is open, and perhaps you get a fine view of the stars. If a star should shoot across the sky and you are watching, and you could have the wish it is supposed to give you, what would you choose for your baby? Just one wish is so difficult. Would you choose health? Or would you decide on happiness, would you risk wealth, knowing that wealth by itself, with no second wish, can be rather a barren offering? Would you like brilliance, and if so what sort? Would you like to have given birth to a genius? Wishing on a star is fun, but fortunately not infallible, for whatever you wish tonight by tomorrow morning you will probably have changed your mind, and really if you come to think of it would you wish at all? Wouldn't you rather have your June baby exactly the way it is?

Noel Streatfeild